CONTEMPORARY'S ACTIVITY-BASED EMPLOYMENT PROGRAM

You're Hired!

Teacher's Guide

Book One: Charting Your Career Path
Book Two: Getting the Right Job

Marilyn Clark
John Mahaffy
Michael St. John
Jan Hart Weihmann

Project Editor
Sarah Conroy

Consultant
Maryann D. Sakamoto
Assistant Principal/Adult Education
Atlantic County Vocational School
Mays Landing, New Jersey

CB
CONTEMPORARY
BOOKS

CHICAGO

Published by Contemporary Books, Inc.
Two Prudential Plaza, Chicago, Illinois 60601-6790
Manufactured in the United States of America
International Standard Book Number: 0-8092-4029-7

Published simultaneously in Canada by
Fitzhenry & Whiteside
195 Allstate Parkway
Markham, Ontario L3R 4T8
Canada

Editorial Director	*Production Assistant*
Caren Van Slyke	Marina Micari
Assistant Editorial Director	*Cover Design*
Mark Boone	Georgene Sainati
Editorial	*Cover Illustrator*
Craig Bolt	Linda Kelen
Betsy Rubin	
Eunice Hoshizaki	*Art & Production*
Jane Samuelson	Carolyn Hopp
Lisa Black	
Lisa Dillman	*Typography*
Esther Johns	Ellen Yukel
Janice Bryant	

Editorial Production Manager
Norma Fioretti

Contents

Overview

About the Series

Developing a successful career requires more than just getting a job. Decisions that lead to a fulfilling career can affect all areas of one's life. To achieve this holistic fulfillment, students need to decide which career is right for them.

You're Hired! helps students make this decision. *Book One: Charting Your Career Path*, helps students make good career choices through analysis of their values, skills, and interests. These concepts are based on John Holland's work with career and vocational choices. *Book Two: Getting the Right Job*, presents a process for finding and keeping a job compatible with career choices. The process includes finding job openings, getting ready to apply, applying, and interviewing for a job. *Book Two* concludes with a unit about getting ahead on the job.

Selecting a career is a very individualized process. Consequently, the *You're Hired!* series allows students to complete activities through independent work. *You're Hired!* is written at about grade-level three, but the concepts presented are both sophisticated and relevant to the field of career development. The series is designed to respect the integrity of adults and to make use of the rich life experiences they bring to the learning environment.

Most students will benefit from completing both books. However, students who have a clearly defined career goal may need only *Book Two*.

About this Teacher's Guide

This guide provides goals and extension activities for each unit in *You're Hired!* Each unit in this guide contains the following elements:

■ **Introduction**—This gives an overview of the unit, including:

    Skills Used—identifies the kinds of skills students will be using

    Comprehensive Adult Student Assessment System (CASAS) objectives—identifies the CASAS objectives addressed in each unit

    Job Training Partnership Act (JTPA) Checklists—identifies the JTPA Checklists and the Department of Labor Pre-Employment/Work Maturity Skills addressed in each unit

    Vocabulary—presents new terms used, which should probably be taught at the start of each unit

■ **Unit Activities**—This provides a brief synopsis of the activities found in the student book unit. Also included are tips and explanations to make the activities more effective.

■ **Group Activity**—This is an optional extension activity that will supplement the student book activities. Blackline masters located in the back of this book accompany most of these group activities.

Using Group Activities

To achieve the student book goals, it is not essential for students to complete the group activities. However, the group activities do offer a number of benefits. Using the group activities will

- supplement the activities and concepts in the student books,

- provide alternative instructional techniques to better accommodate different learning styles,

- provide you with feedback on how well students comprehend the material and where they may be having problems, and

- enable students to gain different perspectives of themselves and their careers through interaction with each other.

As you consider using a group activity, you should

- read through the description of the activity to make sure you understand the goal, the steps involved, and how the activity relates to what students are doing in the student book.

- make sure you have all the materials you need. In some cases, you will need to remind students to bring materials they have worked on in the student book.

- try to time the activity so that it supports work being done in the student book. In some cases, a note at the beginning of the activity will offer guidelines for this.

- be willing to experiment by modifying the activities to fit your situation.

About the Jobs Glossary

Book One, Page 65   The Jobs Glossary contains brief descriptions of more than 150 jobs. Although we have tried to write these job descriptions at the lowest possible reading level, the nature of certain jobs sometimes requires the use of special terminology.

Job titles in the glossary are taken from the *Dictionary of Occupational Titles*, and job descriptions are based on the *Occupational Outlook Handbook*, 1990 edition. Both of these standard references are published by the U.S. Department of Labor.

Jobs listed in the glossary are those in which the demand for workers is expected to continue. Most are entry-level jobs; many require high school or vocational school preparation. A few jobs requiring college-level or graduate school training are listed to demonstrate that certain fields require post–high school training for entry-level positions.

Certificates

Achievement certificates can be given to students when they complete *Book One* and *Book Two*. Blackline masters of these certificates are on pages 51 and 63 of this guide.

Special Note to Teachers

As noted, *You're Hired!* is written at about grade-level three; however, the sophisticated content at times will require much reflection and concentration from the student. To maximize the benefits of this pre-employment program, you may want to dictate text or use assisted reading methods.

In addition, we urge you to complete the activities in the student books yourself. This will help you recognize the pattern and the intensity level of each activity.

Book One provides an introduction to a variety of jobs, but it is by no means an exhaustive list. We suggest you show students a variety of job and career information, such as pamphlets and booklets from career counseling offices, resources from the library, and even descriptions from people you know or members of your community.

If you would like more information about employment and career counseling, consult any of the books listed in the bibliography on page 50 of this book.

Correlation of Contemporary's *You're Hired!* to the CASAS Objectives and JTPA Checklists

Book One: Charting Your Career Path

UNIT		CASAS OBJECTIVES	JTPA CHECKLISTS
Unit One Values	4.1.9	Identify procedures for career planning including self-assessment	A
Unit Two Skills	4.1.8	Identify appropriate skills and education for getting a job in various occupational areas	A
	4.1.9	Identify procedures for career planning including self-assessment	
Unit Three Interests	4.1.9	Identify procedures for career planning including self-assessment	A
Unit Four Careers	4.1.8	Identify appropriate skills and education for getting a job in various occupational areas	A

Correlation of Contemporary's *You're Hired!* to the CASAS Objectives and JTPA Checklists

Book Two: Getting the Right Job

UNIT	CASAS OBJECTIVES		JTPA CHECKLISTS
Unit One Information	4.1.3	Identify and use sources of information about job opportunities such as job descriptions and job ads	A
	4.1.4	Identify and use information about training opportunities	
	4.1.6	Interpret general work-related vocabulary (e.g., experience, swing shift)	
	4.1.8	Identify appropriate skills and education for getting a job in various occupational areas	
Unit Two Job Openings	4.1.3	Identify and use sources of information about job opportunities such as job descriptions and job ads	A
	4.1.6	Interpret general work-related vocabulary (e.g., experience, swing shift)	
	4.1.8	Identify appropriate skills and education for getting a job in various occupational areas	
Unit Three Getting Ready	4.1.2	Interpret job applications, resumes, and letters of application	A, B, C
	4.1.6	Interpret general work-related vocabulary (e.g., experience, swing shift)	
	4.1.8	Identify appropriate skills and education for getting a job in various occupational areas	

UNIT	CASAS OBJECTIVES		JTPA CHECKLISTS
Unit Four Applying	4.1.2	Interpret job applications, resumes, and letters of application	A, D
	4.1.6	Interpret general work-related vocabulary (e.g., experience, swing shift)	
	4.1.8	Identify appropriate skills and education for getting a job in various occupational areas	
Unit Five Interviewing	4.1.5	Recognize standards of behavior for job interviews and select appropriate questions and responses during job interviews	A, E
	4.1.6	Interpret general work-related vocabulary (e.g., experience, swing shift)	
	4.1.8	Identify appropriate skills and education for getting a job in various occupational areas	
Unit Six Success	4.3.3	Identify safe work procedures including wearing safe work attire	F
	4.4.1	Identify appropriate behavior, attitudes, and social interaction for keeping a job and getting a promotion	
	4.4.2	Identify appropriate skills and education for keeping a job and getting a promotion	
	4.4.5	Interpret tasks related to clarifying, giving or providing feedback to instructions; and reacting to criticism	

BOOK ONE:
Charting Your Career Path

Introduction

When people meet for the first time, the central question following an exchange of names is "What do you do?" After finding out *who* someone is, we want to get a handle on *what* someone is. As a result, we quickly make many assumptions about someone we just met. We associate certain personal traits and values with certain types of work. We make a significant connection between values and work.

Students may not understand the relationship between values and work. This unit is designed to help students identify their values and the types of work consistent with those values.

A job that cannot pay the bills might not be acceptable to students, regardless of other benefits. However, if several jobs are available that provide the needed income, decisions become more complicated. Other considerations then become important. For example, jobs demanding much time away from home might be unacceptable to students who value spending time with their families.

A clear sense of values leads to a strong sense of vocational identity. Students often think about their jobs only in terms of what is available—not in terms of what they *want* from work. Work that does not fulfill important values may be unsatisfactory. Although there are many different values, Unit One focuses on three types: personal values, work values, and people values.

Skills Used

Students will be using reading and writing skills in this unit. They will also practice skills in following directions, reflection, evaluation, and decision making.

CASAS Objectives Addressed

4.1.9 Identify procedures for career planning including self-assessment

JTPA Checklists Addressed

Checklist A

Department of Labor Pre-Employment Skills:

1. Making Career Decisions

Vocabulary

The following words are important to the concepts in Unit One, but students may find them unfamiliar or difficult to read. You may wish to teach these words at the start of this unit to help students with the activities.

■ **value**—something that is important to an individual. It may be something tangible, like a house, but more often it is abstract, like the importance of close relationships among family members. The values discussed are only those of individuals, not societal values. Three kinds of values are identified:

personal values—part of a personal belief system that strongly reflects the individual character of the student. The desire to work for a company that helps people in need is an example of a personal value in a work setting.

work values—values that relate to the nature of the work and working conditions. Wanting a job that involves outdoor work is an example of a work value.

people values—how the student prefers to relate to other people. Enjoying many acquaintances but only a few close friends is an example of a people value.

■ **job**—work done for pay. A job might not share a value connection with any aspect of the student's life other than providing needed income.

■ **career**—while it likely includes a job, the concept of *career* is much broader and has a clear connection with other aspects of the student's life and values. The use of *career* is intended to incorporate a student's work, family, community, and spiritual dimensions. A career is chosen because it fits with a student's personal, work, and people values, not just to make money.

■ **summary**—in this series, *summary* refers to a short statement or list of important information or ideas.

◪ Unit One Activities: Tips and Explanations

What Do You Value?

Page 2   **Goal:** Become familiar with three categories of values

Values

Page 3   **Goal:** Read examples of different values

Tom's Story

Page 4

Goal: Read about an adult's conflict of values

For many students, having *any* job is a value in itself. They see a job as a thing separate from themselves and the lives they lead. This story introduces the concept that a career includes making decisions about values and is more than just a job. By first looking at someone else's values, students will feel more comfortable examining their own values.

Students will also answer questions about the story. Answers to questions in *Book One* are at the bottom of the page.

Sorting Out Your Own Values

Pages 6-7

Goal: Decide upon relative importance of one's own values

Each student will need a table (or other flat space) to lay out the cards, which are located on pages 77-91 in *Book One*. Blank cards are provided for any values students wish to add. Students need to complete sorting one deck of cards before continuing to the next deck.

Because it requires reflection, the card sort activity may take considerable time. Students can do the card sort at home if necessary.

If a group of students is doing the card sort, you may wish to follow up with a group discussion in order to help students better understand and make use of the results.

We strongly urge you to complete the card sort activity yourself in order to understand what the students will experience.

Values Summary

Pages 8-9

Goal: Choose the five most important values in each category

This is a good time for individual or small-group interaction or for students to discuss their ideas with classmates, friends, or family. Remind students to respect the personal nature of what is shared in class.

Charting Your Career Path

Page 9

Goal: Transfer important values onto career charts

Throughout *Book One*, students will copy newly learned personal information onto two career charts in Unit Four. Once students have worked up to Unit Four, the career charts will be nearly completed. Students then can proceed to synthesize their values, skills, and interests into a job or career that may fit them best.

Note that there are two charts for students to fill out, on pages 56 and 58 of *Book One*. If a student needs a clean copy of the chart, use the blackline master on pages 59-60 of this guide.

What Have You Learned?

Page 10

Goal: Review and reflect on information learned in Unit One

Students' form of expression is left open-ended. Encourage them to express themselves in ways they find meaningful. You may want to provide magazines and other materials or ask students to bring their own to class.

Group Activity: Values

Goal: Understand the connection between value fulfillment and work satisfaction

Materials
Each student will need

■ one copy each of *Personal Values*, *Work Values*, and *People Values* (Blackline masters of these forms are included on pages 52–54 in this book; you may wish to make transparencies of them.)

■ a pen or pencil

Time Required
This activity will take about 30 minutes. The discussion can be extended as long as it appears to be helping students clarify and understand their values.

Process

It is often helpful to talk about some of your values before asking students to discuss theirs.

1. Discuss the concept of values in general and kinds of values (personal, work, and people) in particular. Explain that values come from parents, upbringing, culture, and different experiences. Point out that not all people have the same values and that there is nothing wrong with this. Ask students to give examples of some values.

Try to use real-life examples of how work and values relate to each other.

2. Explain that to find the kind of work that will best suit each person, it is important to know if the work will fit that person's values. Explain that some values may be very important to them, while others may not. Explain that the goal of this activity is to help them identify their most important values and decide if those values are currently fulfilled in their lives.

Make sure the directions for completing the forms are clear.

3. Hand out the three *Values* forms to the students and instruct them to

   a. place an X by the five values most important to them

   b. rank these top five values on a scale of 1 to 5, with 1 being the most important value

   c. write yes or no next to each of their top five values to indicate whether that value is being fulfilled in their lives at the present time

After demonstrating what to do and answering any questions, have them complete the three forms.

One purpose of the discussion is to encourage members of the group to support each other.

Some students may need help with this activity, but it is important for them to capture values and feelings in their own words.

4. When students have completed the forms, discuss the most important values they selected. The following questions and guidelines may be helpful:

■ *"Were any of you surprised by your choices?"*

■ *"Would any of you like to share the choices you made?"*

■ *"Were the values you selected things you truly valued or things you thought you **should** value?"* If responses indicate that students' choices do not accurately reflect their real values, stress the importance of clarifying their own values. They may wish to go back through the list and make new choices.

■ *"How can your job or career influence whether you fulfill your values?"*

Students may benefit from examples from either your life or the lives of other students. You must be willing to discuss your own values and to be open with students. For instance, why did you choose to become a teacher? What do you like about your job? What values are fulfilled by your work?

SKILLS ■ SKILLS ■ SKILLS ■ SKILLS ■ SKILLS ■ SKILLS

S KILLS
U N I T   T W O

Introduction

In Unit One, students examined the values important to them. In this unit, students look at their skills. Adult students often have a very one-dimensional view of skills related to work. They do not think of the many skills they have acquired from other areas of their lives that can be transferred to work skills. In this unit, students will be asked to think of two types of skills: everyday (transferable) skills and job skills.

Acquiring skills is a lifelong process and covers all areas of a person's life. It is important for students to realize this and to see work skills in the broadest possible way.

It is also important for students to be able to distinguish their competence at a given skill. They may use a skill, but how good are they at using it? Perhaps more important, how much do they *enjoy* using it?

The activities in this unit are very similar to skills inventories used by professional career counselors.

Skills Used

Students will be using reading and writing skills in this unit. They will practice skills in following directions, reflection, and evaluation.

CASAS Objectives Addressed

4.1.8 Identify appropriate skills and education for getting a job in various occupational areas

4.1.9 Identify procedures for career planning including self-assessment

JTPA Checklists Addressed

Checklist A
Department of Labor Pre-Employment Skills:
1. Making Career Decisions

Vocabulary

The following words are important to the concepts in Unit Two, but students may find them unfamiliar or difficult to read. You may wish to teach these words at the start of this unit to help students with the activities.

■ **skill**—something a person does well because of special knowledge and the ability to use that knowledge appropriately. Two kinds of skills are described in this unit:

> **everyday skills**—functional, transferable skills learned through general life experience, including hobbies, interests, family life, and club or church activities. Many of these skills are needed to perform a variety of different kinds of work. Organizing information and following directions are examples of everyday skills.

> **job skills**—skills required for specific jobs and not generally used outside that job. Welding is an example of a job skill. Six occupational categories (clusters into which all jobs and related job skills can be assigned) are referred to as "job families" in *Book One*. These six families were created by John Holland in *The Self-Directed Search*, which can be found as an appendix to *Making Vocational Choices* (see bibliography on page 50). The six families are:

> 1. **Realistic**—Jobs in this family involve working with tools or machines. The work may be outdoors but is often manual in nature. These jobs include mechanic, construction worker, and wildlife worker.

> 2. **Investigative**—Jobs in this family involve solving problems, finding out about things, doing detail work, and following through on a task. These jobs include tax preparer, laboratory technician, and drafter.

> 3. **Artistic**—Jobs in this family involve creativity and self-expression. They often involve working alone. These jobs include singer, graphic artist, and photographer.

> 4. **Social**—Jobs in this family involve working with people more than with things. They typically require concern for others and a desire to help. These jobs include teacher aide, counselor, and probation officer.

> 5. **Enterprising**—Jobs in this family involve leading people or selling them things or ideas. These jobs often require energy, confidence, and a preference for working with big plans instead of small details. Jobs in this family include flight attendant and real estate agent.

> 6. **Conventional**—Jobs in this family are clearly defined and often involve detailed and routine work. They often require the ability to follow directions well and to be dependable. These jobs include billing clerk and secretary.

Unit Two Activities: Tips and Explanations

What Are Your Everyday Skills?

Pages 12-13 **Goal:** Discover one's best functional transferable skills (everyday skills)

Functional transferable skills are skills required to deal with the basics of everyday life. It is very important for students to recognize these skills and to see their relevance to the workplace. This will help build students' self-esteem. Encourage students to add everyday skills of their choice to the list.

Charting Your Career Path

Page 13 **Goal:** Transfer best everyday skills onto career charts

José's Story

Pages 14-15 **Goal:** Read about an adult transferring everyday skills to a career

This guided story will help students become more familiar with the concept of transferable everyday skills.

Students will answer questions about the story, and will expand upon their own everyday skills. You might also have students discuss their answers with others in the class.

What Job Skills Do You Have?

Pages 16-17 **Goal:** Become familiar with six job skills clusters (job families) in preparation for the job skills activity

The six occupational categories used in this series (realistic, investigative, artistic, social, enterprising, and conventional) are based on those developed by John Holland, Ph.D. Each category contains specific skill clusters such as communication, medical, and mechanical skills. These skills clusters are referred to in resources such as the *Occupational Outlook Handbook*.

What Are Your Best Job Skills?

Pages 18-29 **Goal:** Explore a broad range of job skills and rank the satisfaction gained from using those skills

This inventory will stimulate students to think more broadly about their skills and career options. Encourage students to look at each list of skills, even if the cluster title looks unfamiliar to them. Mechanical skills, for example, are found in many jobs other than auto repair.

Many of the skills listed in the inventory are general skills. This will encourage each student to evaluate each skill within his or her own frame of reference. Such an open-ended look at their skills will be a positive experience for students.

It is important that students rate each skill according to their first reaction. This instant reaction is often the best gauge of true feelings.

Many students will find that this activity works best if they focus on skills used in past jobs. However, students with little work experience may have trouble relating to a list of job skills if they have not worked at a paying job. Encourage them to consider skills used in volunteer work, in the home, with groups, or anywhere they have performed a "job" even though not for pay.

Note that some skills, such as *follow directions*, are listed more than once within a specific job family. If a student has checked a skill repeatedly, count each check mark as part of the job skills tally. Be sure that students clearly understand how to use the tally boxes. They will refer to these boxes later in *Book One*.

Job Skills Summary

Pages 30–31   **Goal:** Focus on best and most enjoyed skills in two job families

Students will focus on the two job families in which they enjoy the most skills. These two families are likely to have the most suitable jobs for them.

If there is a tie on Step 1, encourage students to choose the two job families they feel best about—based on how much they enjoy the skills in that family.

Charting Your Career Path

Page 32   **Goal:** Transfer best job skills onto career charts. Be sure that students keep one job family on each chart.

Job Skills History

Page 33   **Goal:** Reflect on when and where best skills have been used

This activity is intended to build students' self-confidence about their abilities. The dates and places do not have to be exact. This information will also be useful in *Book Two* when students construct their resumes.

It may be helpful for you to demonstrate one or two examples to the class, to ensure that students understand the process.

What Have You Learned?

Page 34   **Goal:** Evaluate and reflect on work done in Unit Two

Students' form of expression is left open-ended. Encourage them to express themselves in ways they find meaningful. You may want to provide magazines and other materials or ask students to bring their own to class.

◘ Group Activity: Skills

Goal: Identify skills by reflecting on past achievements

Note: Conduct this Group Activity after students have completed the everyday skills and job skills activities in Unit Two.

This activity will give students new insights into their skills through the involvement of other students. It will help them build self-esteem and self-confidence. The skills identified may also seem more meaningful because they are drawn from students' own experiences. Many of these skills are likely to be everyday skills that may be transferred to the workplace; some may be specific work skills.

It is a good idea to check in advance to be sure students have all materials ready before scheduling this activity.

Materials
Each student will need

■ a completed checklist of everyday skills (*Book One*, page 12)

■ a summary list of everyday skills (page 13)

■ a completed Job Skills Summary (pages 30–31)

■ three copies of *Personal Accomplishment* (A blackline master of this form is on page 55 of this book.)

■ a pen or pencil

Time Required
This activity will take at least 60 minutes. The amount of time required will vary according to the number of students participating.

Process
1. Explain that this activity will help students identify even more of their everyday and job skills and will affirm the ones they have already identified. Tell students that one way to identify their skills is to look at the things they do well—accomplishments and achievements—and at the times when they are successful.

Try to use examples that are not too intimidating.

For example, you might tell about taking a group of Scouts camping. Some key skills you used were planning, organizing, and getting along well with others.

2. Illustrate this concept with an example. It may be best to use an achievement in your own life. Briefly describe the story of your achievement to the class, providing useful details to add interest and to help students pick out the skills that helped make it possible.

Ask students to identify some of the skills that might have been required. Volunteer one or two examples of skills to get the discussion started. Carry out this discussion until all skills have been identified. Explain that this process may be a useful way for students to identify their own skills.

Some students may have difficulty thinking of specific examples. You can help by suggesting that they consider different aspects of their lives: families, jobs, hobbies, or organizations to which they belong.

Encourage students to write down things mentioned during the discussion that seem applicable to their lives.

Try to probe for all the skills that apply; students need to be encouraged about their own abilities.

3. Form small groups of three to five students each. Ask students to think about events or situations in their own lives that they are proud of. These could be specific achievements, like the one you described, or broader accomplishments, such as raising children well.

Ask students to select at least three accomplishments and to write each one briefly on a separate copy of the *Personal Accomplishment* form. Next, ask students to list on each form the skills that helped them succeed with that accomplishment. Encourage them to refer to the completed skill identification activities (pages 12–13, 30–31).

4. Ask each student to choose one accomplishment to describe to the small group. Explain that the presenter will describe an accomplishment and then will point out the skills he or she believes made it possible. Other students in the group can ask questions and discuss each presentation.

Group members should also discuss additional skills they believe each presenter exhibited. The presenter should write down these ideas, too.

5. Reconvene the class. Conduct a group discussion to help students reflect upon what they have learned from the activity. Here are some questions that may facilitate the discussion:

■ *"Would any of you like to comment on the activity you just completed?"*

■ *"Did you find some of the same skills in your accomplishments that you had on your lists?"*

■ *"Did you find some new skills that were not on your lists?"*

■ *"Did your accomplishments require more skills than you first thought?"*

■ *"How did this experience make you feel about yourself?"*

6. Conclude the Group Activity by emphasizing that as adults we all have accomplished many things and have gained knowledge and skills in the process. Explain that sometimes we do not understand the significance of what we have learned, what we can do, and how we can use these skills to help us advance in our careers; however, recognizing our skills is the first step.

INTERESTS
U N I T   T H R E E

Introduction

In Units One and Two, students learned how values and skills relate to career choices. This unit deals with an equally important dimension—interests. Interest plays a strong role in the kinds of jobs students will enjoy and pursue.

In many cases, adult students will emphasize that having any job is good enough. They may have experienced unemployment or poverty and will not always consider their own interests to be important. Also, dislocated workers or displaced homemakers may be desperate to get a job—any job—to be self-sufficient.

Studies show that jobs that meet our interests are most likely to be the ones we find satisfying and are the ones we will stick with. Students need to learn about their employment interests and to take them into account in any long-term career decisions. Many obvious factors are affected by interest:

motivation—people will strive to do better on a job they like, even though pay or other benefits may not be as good as those provided on another job.

promotion opportunities—people who do not enjoy what they do are not likely to get promotions.

keeping a job—job retention is enhanced if people like the work and find it interesting.

We strongly recommend that students do the Group Activity on pages 16–17 in this book *before* they begin working on Unit Three. In the student book, students look only at job interests. The Group Activity, however, helps students explore everyday interests; it is a much more open look at what students find interesting. Students who do not do the activity will have only job interests to work with.

A follow-up activity provided in this Teacher's Guide helps students pull the two types of interests together.

Skills Used

Students will be using reading and writing skills in this unit. They will also use skills in following directions, critical thinking, reflection, and evaluation.

CASAS Objectives Addressed

4.1.9 Identify procedures for career planning including self-assessment

JTPA Checklists Addressed

Checklist A
Department of Labor Pre-Employment Skills:
1. Making Career Decisions

Vocabulary

The following words are important to the concepts in Unit Three, but students may find them unfamiliar and difficult to read. You may wish to teach these words at the start of this unit to help students with the activities.

■ **interest**—something that is appealing. Interests are specific to individuals, but generally they are activities or concepts that students find appealing and attractive. Students can identify their interests by finding what they enjoy spending time and energy pursuing. Two kinds of interests are identified:

> **everyday interests**—things outside of work. Hobbies are an example of everyday interests.

> **job interests**—specific kinds of work students might like to pursue.

■ **glossary**—a list of terms, usually pertaining to a specific topic, and their meanings. A glossary is generally appended to the document in which the terms are used.

■ **interest inventory**—a checklist of jobs on which students rate their levels of interest in each job.

■ **thermometer**—an instrument for measuring temperature—how hot or cold something is.

◨ Unit Three Activities: Tips and Explanations

Anna's Story
Page 36

Goal: Read about an adult taking a job interest inventory

The story models the process students use in this unit. Students also learn about counseling services and interest inventories. You should provide information about such services in your own area.

Thinking About Anna's Choices
Page 37

Goal: Become familiar with interest inventory evaluation

The first thermometer should be nearly completely shaded; the second, shaded about half way.

Questions About Anna's Job Interests
Page 38

Goal: Assess Anna's inventory evaluation

This might also be a good time for students to talk about their own experiences and the feelings triggered by Anna's story.

Just for Fun

Page 39

Goal: Strengthen awareness of everyday skills vocabulary

Students are asked to find at least five words. The solution is shown below:

I	D	E	A	S	S	K	I	L	L	S
Q	N	N	Z	L	I	S	T	E	N	V
P	X	F	M	E	M	T	H	I	N	K
G	W	N	O	A	C	A	R	E	E	R
J	H	U	N	R	I	S	K	D	T	X
K	O	M	E	N	M	B	Z	E	I	Y
K	Z	B	Y	T	E	A	C	H	M	T
V	P	E	O	P	L	E	Z	E	E	Y
C	A	R	E	F	U	L	X	L	Q	R
Y	T	S	B	H	G	V	W	P	L	A

What Jobs Sound Good to You?

Pages 40-47

Goal: Evaluate level of interest in given jobs

This individual interest inventory will expand students' awareness of a wide variety of jobs and, at the same time, encourage them to begin focusing on jobs they may want to explore in greater depth. This exploration occurs in *Book Two*.

Students will consider brief lists of job titles in at least two job families. The job families they explore will be the ones that best fit their skills based on work done in Unit Two. However, you may want to encourage students to look at each job list in the inventory. This will acquaint them with many different jobs.

They will rate their levels of interest in each job, according to how appealing the job title sounds to them. This free-association method is consistent with methods used by job counselors. It is most effective when students work quickly, without pausing.

Of course, there will be job titles for which students will not know the content of the work. Encourage them to rate the job anyway; they will benefit most from the inventory if they complete it without referring to other materials. A Jobs Glossary, which has not yet been introduced to students, begins on page 65 of *Book One* (see page v in this book for further description of the glossary). If you feel strongly that students require the glossary to complete the inventory, show them how to use the glossary. Offer to discuss what you know about the job after the activity is completed.

Regarding the jobs listed in the inventory:

■ Titles are drawn from the U.S. Department of Labor's *Dictionary of Occupational Titles*, 1990 edition.

■ A sampling of jobs was chosen to represent the Holland categories (see page 7 in this book for an explanation of the Holland categories).

■ Jobs selected require, in most instances, relatively low levels of formal education at the entry level.

■ The employment outlook for jobs selected is expected to remain about the same (1990 levels) or to increase, assuring that students have reasonable prospects for securing employment.

■ More than 150 job titles are listed.

Process

1. Explain the purpose of the job interest inventory, broadly covering the points listed above.

2. Encourage students to rate their interest in each job based on their first reaction to the job title. The first impression will often be the most accurate and therefore the most useful to the student.

3. Students will self-interpret results of the inventory using a thermometer to represent degrees of interest in jobs.

Be sure that students understand how to use the thermometer on each page: fully shaded indicates many YES and MAYBE checks in a job family; little shaded indicates few checks in a job family.

For more information about jobs, see the *Dictionary of Occupational Titles* or the *Occupational Outlook Handbook*. Your state has an Occupational Information Coordinating Council that may have additional resource materials that will help you explain work content to students. Your school's career counseling office is another good resource.

Rating Your Job Interests

Pages 48-49   **Goal:** Find the two job families with the most interesting jobs

Materials
scissors   a pen or pencil
                              OR
glue or transparent tape

As students work on this activity, or after they complete it, encourage them to look in the Jobs Glossary for jobs that interest them.

Deciding on Your Job Interests

Page 50   **Goal:** Select three top jobs from the top two job families

Students may use the Jobs Glossary on page 65. Encourage students who have identified only one job family to select more than three job choices in that job family.

Charting Your Career Path

Page 51

Goal: Transfer top job interests on career charts

It is essential that the job families marked #1 and #2 on the charts (pages 56 and 58) match students' Job Family #1 and Job Family #2 on page 50. If the job families do not match, follow these steps:

1. Copy the blackline master (pages 59–60 of this book) and give student a clean copy of the chart.

2. Have student copy the Values and Everyday Skills entries from the old chart.

3. Have student copy the name of the new job family (Job Family #1 or #2 from page 50 of *Book One*) onto the top of the new chart. Then, have student copy the top three job interests for that family onto the chart.

4. Student must take another look at the skills used in this new job family. Have student complete the job skill list for that job family (found between pages 20 and 29). Student then lists the circled skills on page 31 and chooses the four best skills listed.

5. Have student copy these four best skills for the new job family onto the new chart. Now, all skills and interests should be within one job family.

What Have You Learned?

Page 52

Goal: Review and evaluate material learned in Unit Three

You may want to discuss students' responses or concerns, how to research jobs, or what steps to take next.

Group Activity: Interests

Goal: Identify everyday interests; relate them to occupational interest areas

Note: This Group Activity is strongly recommended and should be done *before* students begin working on Unit Three.

This activity provides indirect support for the interest activities in the student book. Rather than directly addressing job interests, this activity helps students freely identify everyday interests in various areas of their lives and see how these might suggest career or job interests.

Students will identify their interests through their own wishes, experiences, and attractions. They then will intuitively connect these interests to possible job interests. The only important connection is the one perceived by the student, however logical or illogical it may seem to anyone else. An added benefit of this Group Activity is the insight gained from the expressed perceptions of the teacher and other students.

Materials
Each student will need

■ a pencil or pen

■ one copy of each *My Interests* form (Blackline masters of these forms are included on pages 56–58 in this book.)

Time Required
This activity will take about 45 minutes. If possible, allow more time for discussion. Continue the discussion as long as it appears to be helpful to students.

Process

1. Ask students to think about the job they have now or one they have held. How and why did they come to have that job? What influenced them to apply for or accept that job instead of another one?

   After students have talked about their job choices, discuss some of the decision-making processes they described. Point out how these processes were related (or not related) to their values, skills, and everyday interests. (Examples of everyday interests might include crafts such as woodworking or pottery, children's activities such as 4-H or Cub Scouts, or different kinds of volunteer activities.) For example, they may have taken jobs whose schedules allowed time for these interests.

2. Now, introduce the concept of everyday interests. Discuss the value of connecting these interests with similar job interests. Mention how difficult it can be to pinpoint both types of interests.

   Tell students that one way to discover our everyday interests is to consider things we think about and things we like to do. Still another way is by observing other people doing things that appeal to us. Ask students what kinds of things other people might observe about them, and what interests they might infer from those observations.

3. Explain that this activity may help students clarify their everyday interests.

   Pass out the *My Interests* forms and go through them with students, making sure instructions are clear. Introduce these concepts:

   ■ Wishes—daydreams, fantasies, things students may never expect to come true

   ■ Activities—experiences students find enjoyable or rewarding

   ■ Attractions—people whom students admire, activities students enjoy, and jobs that seem appealing

   Tell the students that after they have completed the forms, individual responses will be discussed on a volunteer basis only. Ask them to complete the forms.

It is often helpful to share some information about your own work history before asking students to volunteer.

Listen carefully to the students' stories, perhaps taking notes, so you can refer back to examples during your discussion.

Take time to be sure students understand how interests are different from values and skills.

Also, point out that this activity is about everyday interests, but that it may give them ideas about job interests.

Students should try to complete one item in each area or may complete all of the items if they wish.

Students may be tempted to give light-hearted responses to some items. Remind them of the importance of answering thoughtfully.

Take one response from a student and move on. Come back to students for additional responses if time allows.

Advise students to make notes about other ideas they have or comments made by other students.

4. After students have finished, discuss some of the responses and perceptions. Remind the group that interests are neither good nor bad and to avoid making judgments about other students' interests. Instead, they should think about where such interests could lead.

The following suggestions may be helpful in leading the discussion:

■ Ask for input from the group, including ideas about jobs that would fit this interest.

■ Be sure everyone who wants to be involved has a chance; encourage all students to read at least one response.

■ Emphasize the possible implications of student interests.

Continue until everyone has had a chance to contribute. End the discussion by emphasizing how other areas of our lives, such as everyday interests, can provide insights to career choices.

Group Discussion for Closure

Goal: Help students relate the results of the activities in the student book with those of the Group Activity

The preceding Group Activity helped students understand the connections between their everyday interests and possible jobs or careers. Unit Three activities have helped students identify more specific job-related interests. Since this discussion will relate the two activities, it must follow completion of the student book Unit Three and the Group Activity.

The following suggestions may help you organize the discussion:

■ Ask students to bring *Book One* and their completed copies of the *My Interests* forms to the discussion session.

■ Tell the group that you think it would be helpful to take some time (about 30 minutes) to talk about what they have learned about their everyday interests and their job interests. Ask them to review the interests summary in the student book (page 50) and their completed *My Interests* forms. Tell them to look especially for similarities between what they identified as job interests in the student book and what they identified as everyday interests in the Group Activity.

■ When they have finished the review, ask if anyone found anything surprising—especially similarities but perhaps differences as well. Encourage students to talk about their interests and how they see them connecting with jobs. Hearing what another student has to say can stimulate insights from other members of the group.

■ Point out relationships, ideas, or possibilities that you see but that are not mentioned by other students. Discourage impressions about what might be "good" or "bad" interests. Also avoid impressions that certain interests mean someone *should* pursue a certain job or is only *capable* of doing certain kinds of work. While this discussion is designed to help students clarify and focus their interests, it is not meant to impose perceived limitations.

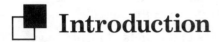

CAREERS
UNIT FOUR

◪ Introduction

In this final unit of *Book One*, students make some broad career decisions: the kind of job they want, what stops them from getting that kind of job, how to overcome that barrier, and what to do next. Upon completion of this unit, students should have a very good understanding of career choices as they relate to skills, interests, values, and barriers.

This unit helps students continue the career decision-making process. Students are not required to make a final job choice; instead, they will identify some jobs or career areas to explore. This information will prepare students for the activities in *Book Two*—researching specific occupations and taking positive steps toward setting and attaining career goals.

In this unit, students will learn much more about analyzing the skills, interests, and values they identified in the first three units. Unit Four will help students pull this information together, determine what it means to them, and develop a clearer vision of how and where to proceed toward their career path.

Some students may still need more help in synthesizing this information into a career direction. For these students, it is important that you identify and use additional resources. Some useful job inventories are noted in the reference section. Also, career planning and placement services at community colleges and government agencies are often available at little or no cost. No single set of materials or classroom activities will meet the needs of all students.

Skills Used

Students will be using writing and reading skills. They will also use vocabulary, analytical, and synthesizing skills.

CASAS Objectives Addressed

4.1.8 Identify appropriate skills and education for getting a job in various occupational areas

JTPA Checklists Addressed

Checklist A

Department of Labor Pre-Employment Skills:

1. Making Career Decisions

Vocabulary

The following words are important to the concepts in Unit Four, but students may find them unfamiliar and difficult to read. You may wish to teach these words at the start of this unit to help students with the activities.

■ **barrier**—an obstacle preventing a student from taking effective action toward a goal or even being willing to seriously consider working toward the goal. Two kinds of barriers are noted:

internal, or **inside**, barriers—thoughts and beliefs students have about what stops them from going ahead. These may be rational and real—"I am too old to become a fire fighter"—or even irrational—"I am too dumb to learn." Though irrational, such barriers seem very real to students.

external, or **outside**, barriers—external forces or conditions that affect a student's action. For example, not having a GED or high school diploma is a barrier to the goal of getting a nursing aide's job. Outside barriers, like inside barriers, can be overcome.

■ **strength**—a skill, knowledge, or some other quality a student can use to overcome barriers and achieve goals.

 # Unit Four Activities: Tips and Explanations

Which Jobs Fit You Best?

Pages 54–59

Goal: Synthesize values, skills, and interests

Students will evaluate how well their job interests match their values and skills. After completing this activity, students will have up to three jobs in two job families they'd like to learn more about. These jobs will provide a starting point for *Book Two.*

Students will shade in circles to represent their feelings and views. However, because the process is complex and might be confusing to some students, you should be ready to help them get started correctly. If students would like to include a third job family, copy the blackline masters of the charts on pages 59–60 of this book.

Barriers and Strengths

Page 60

Goal: Understand the concepts of barriers and strengths and explain their relationship

Students need to view barriers as normal, not prohibitive, and to see that they can overcome barriers through strengths. Most of all, students should not let the perception of a barrier stop them from taking action.

Discuss strengths and internal and external barriers. You might want to spend more time with the class discussing the distinctions between internal and external barriers, using the students' own examples.

Marvin's Story

Pages 61–62

Goal: Read about an adult who faces barriers to his career goal and identifies his strengths

This story illustrates the fact that many people face barriers to achieving their goals and that barriers are just problems to be solved.

Students will answer questions about the story, and will consider how the story character uses his strengths to overcome his barriers and achieve his goals.

Know Your Barriers and Strengths

Page 63

Goal: Consider personal barriers and strengths

The strengths that others point out to a student will not only add to that student's self-knowledge but will likely build self-esteem as well.

What Have You Learned?

Page 64

Goal: Reflect on what has been learned in *Book One* and consider ideas about the future

This is the culminating activity for *Book One*. Students have identified several jobs they would like to explore. They have also considered what barriers may stand in their way. Encourage students to express themselves in whatever ways they desire. In addition to writing their thoughts and feelings, they can express themselves graphically by drawing or by creating a collage.

Some students may find this kind of synthesizing exercise difficult. Stress how important it is for them to express what they really think and feel about their futures. Remind them that the work they do is confidential unless they choose to share it with others.

Certificate
Blackline Master

You may wish to recognize the completion of *Book One* with an award. You may choose an award of your own or use the certificate included as a blackline master on page 51 of this guide.

Group Activity: Which Job Fits You Best?

Goal: Synthesize values, skills, and interests and determine appealing job and career directions

Note: This Group Activity is strongly recommended and should be done *after* students have completed Unit Four.

This activity asks students to see patterns and relationships among the values, skills, and interests they have previously identified. This process is largely intuitive and cannot be reduced to mechanically completing a set of steps. The "Aha!" realization is very personal.

Students have two sources to help develop insights about how this information fits together. First, they reflect upon and talk about the relationships they perceive. Second, other students, looking at the same information, offer their perceptions.

This Group Activity can offer perspectives that may trigger new insights. As the instructor, your perspective is quite valuable, so you should try to work with the small groups of students.

Materials
Each student will need

Students may wish to have all the work they have done in *Book One* available for reference.

■ completed charts on pages 56-59 from *Book One*

■ one copy of *Which Jobs Fit You Best?* (There are two blackline masters of this form: a sample on page 61, and a blank one on page 62.) Students can either use the form as is, or they can use it as a rough draft and copy the information onto a large sheet of paper such as newsprint. Students will need to complete a final copy of this form.

■ a large sheet of paper, such as newsprint

■ if newsprint is used, provide markers and tape

■ a pen or pencil

Time Required
This activity will take a total of about 60 minutes. After students have completed the forms, each student will need about 10 minutes to discuss his or her situation.

Process

Students can choose any values and skills they wish. Their three "interests" will probably be selected from the job interests they listed on pages 56-59 in the student book.

You may need to point out that these job choices do not represent final decisions or commitment about jobs they are going to pursue.

1. Ask students to copy some information from the charts on pages 56-59 in *Book One* onto *Which Jobs Fit You Best?*

   Tell students they can choose jobs from either job family and can choose any of their values, skills, and interests to include on the form. They need not have one of each kind of value. But they should try to list three each of values, skills, and interests.

2. Next, students should each think of five jobs that (1) interest them, (2) use skills they enjoy or would like to learn, and (3) fit their important values. Rather than repeating jobs listed in the Interests circle, students can use those jobs as a springboard to help them think of other jobs to list. Students may choose these jobs in any way that makes sense to them. However, suggest they choose jobs that intuitively seem right and then think about how well those jobs fit the above criteria.

   Ask students to write these five jobs in the lines entitled Jobs on the *Which Jobs Fit You Best?* form.

Check to make sure everyone understands what to do before proceeding.

3. Since the format for this group process can get confusing, demonstrate how the process works. Complete a *Which Jobs Fit You Best?* form and present it to the class. Have the discussion just as it is to be done in the small group. You may want to use the completed *Which Jobs Fit You Best?* sample form (page 61 in this book) or make one of your own.

Divide the class into groups of four. Explain that students can choose to present their completed *Which Jobs Fit You Best?* form to other members of the group. The presenter should point out the jobs listed and how those jobs blend with the values, skills, and interests listed. Other members of the group should ask questions, discuss what has been presented, and make suggestions about other jobs the presenter might consider. The presenter should write these ideas on the form.

Try to space student groups so they do not interfere with each other.

You may want to mention that in *Book Two* students will learn how to further explore their career ideas.

4. Reconvene the class for a group discussion. Ask if anyone got good ideas from the small-group process. Continue to discuss issues important to the students. Be ready to have the class offer feedback on an individual's *Which Jobs Fit You Best?* form, if that seems appropriate.

To end the discussion, suggest that students continue to think about the information on their forms and perhaps discuss it with friends or family.

BOOK TWO:
Getting the Right Job

🌓 Introduction

In *Book One: Charting Your Career Path*, students were guided through a series of self-awareness activities to help them understand their values, skills, and interests and see how to relate these attributes to a career choice. At the completion of *Book One*, students should have identified one or more fairly specific job areas of interest.

In this book, students will pursue more information about these jobs as possible career paths. They will learn the process of researching, locating, and applying for a job. Students beginning *Book Two* need not have completed *Book One*, but they *do* need to have identified at least one job interest.

Unit One introduces students to the first steps of finding the right job. Students will investigate the facts about a particular job; then they will compare the facts with their previous impressions about that job. This will help them avoid pursuing an idealized notion of a job. After careful analysis, students may drop their interest in jobs that emerged as possibilities in *Book One*. The jobs that still hold their interest, however, will serve as the focus for the rest of the book.

Students will gain self-confidence as well as a specific job interest in this unit. They will develop confidence in the quality of the decisions they are making. They will also feel in control: they will be making informed decisions, not just taking what they can get. Further, students should realize that the process they are learning can be used whenever they need it.

Skills Used

Students will be using reading and writing skills in this unit. They will use investigation and reflection skills as well as the critical-thinking skills of analysis and evaluation.

CASAS Objectives Addressed

4.1.3 Identify and use sources of information about job opportunities such as job descriptions and job ads

4.1.4 Identify and use information about training opportunities

4.1.6 Interpret general work-related vocabulary (e.g., experience, swing shift)

4.1.8 Identify appropriate skills and education for getting a job in various occupational areas

JTPA Checklists Addressed

Checklist A

Department of Labor Pre-Employment Skills:
1. Making Career Decisions
2. Using Labor Market Information

Vocabulary

The following words used in Unit One are important to the concepts presented, but students may find them unfamiliar and difficult to read. You may wish to teach these words at the start of this unit to help students with the activities.

- **benefits**—medical, dental, injury, life insurance, and pension or retirement plans provided by an employer

- **employment service**—a government agency that provides job-hunting services free of charge. Often called the job service, it lists local job openings and apprenticeship programs.

- **occupation**—a job or career. The word is introduced in reference to the *Occupational Outlook Handbook*.

- **resource**—a source of information or expertise. In this series, the term refers to sources of job and career information.

- **school job placement office**—often called a career planning and placement center, this office is usually located at trade and technical schools, community colleges, colleges, and universities. A placement office lists job openings, provides job counseling, and helps people plan their job searches. As a rule, only students and recent graduates can use the services of career placement offices.

- **working conditions**—the working environment and tasks involved in performing a job

◖ Unit One Activities: Tips and Explanations

Juan's Story

Pages 2–3

Goal: Read about an adult exploring job interests

The story models many of the steps that students will take in Unit One.

Students will also answer questions about the story. Answers to these and all objective questions in *Book Two* are on the bottom of the page. No answers are given for open-ended questions.

What I Want in a Job

Pages 4–5

Goal: Establish specific job wants and needs

This is a series of very real questions about what students want out of a job. It might be a good idea to spend a few minutes discussing the questions with the whole class. Though intended to be answered individually, the questions can be used effectively as a group activity.

Resources

Pages 6–7

Goal: Learn about sources of job information

Students will also answer questions about their resources. These questions should make the idea of resources more concrete to students.

Students may have trouble reading the resource books listed. It would be helpful for you to poll students on their job interests and bring to class different books and materials about those jobs. You could then help them read the information. In addition, you may want to provide the addresses of some of these resources.

Field trips are also a good way to familiarize students with sources of job information.

Finding Out About a Job

Pages 8–9

Goal: Become familiar with using other people as job-information resources

Using Resources to Learn More

Pages 10–11

Goal: Understand how to use the public library as a job-information resource

Because many students are not comfortable using the library, you should encourage them to ask the staff for help. You might want to conduct a group discussion on using the library or even go there on a field trip.

Getting Closer to a Job Decision

Pages 12–13

Goal: Become familiar with using an employer as a job-information resource

In the story, the character's research leads him to change job interests. This is likely to happen to students as well.

What This Job Is All About

Pages 14–15

Goal: Research and answer specific questions about a job interest

If students have completed *Book One*, they should have one or two jobs to investigate. If not, students may have to use the Jobs Glossary (*Book One*, page 65) to find jobs that interest them. This research might take students several days and will likely require your help.

When they finish the assignment, you may want to photocopy students' answers and post them or put them into a class Job Resources Notebook for all to share.

Just for Fun

Page 16

Goal: Strengthen awareness of job-related vocabulary

The answers are shown below.

Barriers

Page 17

Goal: Understand the concept of barriers

Is This the Job for You?

Pages 18–19

Goal: Compare job needs with facts about a job, and consider barriers

This is a very difficult exercise for many students. The NO answer is problematic: it may mean that it is not the right job for the student, or it may mean that the student will have to make decisions about overcoming barriers. A class discussion is often very helpful in understanding how to overcome barriers. This is also a good time to cite examples of people who have made successful career changes.

Putting It All Together

Page 20

Goal: Reflect on work done in Unit One, and consider overcoming barriers

Students will consider barriers to getting a certain job and will write ways of overcoming these barriers in the road signs. You may want to post the completed road maps.

◐ Group Activity: Talking About Jobs

Goal: Expand knowledge of different kinds of jobs, and practice interview skills

In this activity, students will interview each other about particular jobs and work experiences they have had. As students work together, they will learn the positive and negative aspects of various jobs. This may help give them perspective about jobs they are considering. Students will also gain experience in obtaining job-related information through an interview format—a skill that will help them in their own job explorations.

Students will learn about a variety of jobs without leaving the security of the classroom. You can photocopy and post the results of interviews for students to review. Even though a student's job interest may not be among those posted, it should be helpful to read about a variety of jobs.

Materials
Each student will need

■ a pencil or pen

■ one copy of *Job Information* (A blackline master of this form is included on page 64 in this book.)

Time Required
This activity will take from 30 to 45 minutes. Each interview and discussion should take 10 to 15 minutes.

Process

1. Ask students to think about the most meaningful or memorable job they have had, paid or unpaid. For instance, it could be their first job, the job they enjoyed the most, or a family or volunteer duty.

2. Form groups of three students each. One student will be the interviewer, the second the interviewee, and the third the observer.

   Student 1 selects his or her most meaningful job and prepares to be interviewed.

   Student 2 interviews student 1, using the *Job Information* form as a question guide and to record information.

   Student 3 serves as an observer, carefully watching and listening to the questions asked and the responses given.

3. Following the interview, students should discuss how the interview went and what they learned about the job.

4. Repeat the interview and discussion process two more times, changing roles each time so that each student can perform each role.

5. Reconvene the class. Ask volunteers to describe the interview and what they learned from it. Conduct a group discussion about the positive and negative aspects of different jobs. Discuss how this new information might affect how they interview for a job.

Tell students to keep their completed *Job Information* forms. They may want to use some of the questions on the form to help them find out about their job interests.

You may want to pair students up according to types of jobs chosen.

It may be helpful to demonstrate the interview process (including the role of the observer and the postinterview discussion) for the class.

Suggest that the interviewer read aloud the information just recorded. The other two can comment on accuracy.

It is important to help students see the connection between this exercise and using the interview process to learn about jobs that interest them.

JOB OPENINGS●JOB OPENINGS●JOB OPENINGS●JOB OPENINGS●JOB OPENINGS

JOB OPENINGS
U N I T T W O

◑ Introduction

After students complete Unit One, they should be ready to take action. Self-awareness, initial career choices, and further investigation have led to affirmation of a solid job interest. In Unit Two, students will begin the actual process of getting the job of their choice. Many students, of course, are not yet ready to actually seek employment at this time. They can use the lessons in this book as a "dress rehearsal" for an actual job search.

For students who *are* ready to make a career move, this unit will bring an added sense of reality to the process that has brought them to this point. The link between choices and consequences will seem more tangible now that they are beginning an actual job search.

Throughout the rest of this book—as in a real-life job search—students may risk their self-esteem. You must provide support and reassurance. Remind them that they are in control of the process and will not be required to do anything they are not ready or willing to do.

Fellow students will also provide support, particularly through the group activities. It may be reassuring for students to practice with their peers and to know that others have feelings similar to theirs.

Skills Used

Students will be using reading and writing skills in this unit. They will also use communication, research, and analytical skills. They will begin to build a network of job contacts.

CASAS Objectives Addressed

4.1.3 Identify and use sources of information about job opportunities such as job descriptions and job ads

4.1.6 Interpret general work-related vocabulary (e.g., experience, swing shift)

4.1.8 Identify appropriate skills and education for getting a job in various occupational areas

JTPA Checklists Addressed

Checklist A
Department of Labor Pre-Employment Skills:
1. Making Career Decisions
2. Using Labor Market Information

Vocabulary

The following words used in Unit Two are important to the concepts presented, but students may find them unfamiliar and difficult to read. You may wish to teach these words at the start of this unit to help students with the activities.

■ **job openings**—positions that are available and can be applied for

■ **network**—a series of personal contacts used to learn and exchange information about jobs

■ **want ads**—found in the classified advertisement section in newspapers, these ads describe jobs that are available

◐ Unit Two Activities: Tips and Explanations

Juan's Story
Pages 22-23

Goal: Read about an adult locating job openings

Questions about the story ask students to identify the job-opening information presented in the story.

Your Network
Page 24

Goal: Become familiar with networks and network cards

Using a Network Card
Pages 25-26

Goal: Learn how to use a network and network cards

Start Your Network
Page 27

Goal: Begin a network for a job interest

At this point, students should begin working with a specific job interest, preferably the interest solidified in Unit One.

If students prefer not to buy index cards, they can use photocopies of *Network Sheet*, a blackline master located on page 65 of this book.

Contacting Employers Directly
Page 28

Goal: Become familiar with the yellow pages and with employer networks

Students may have trouble using the phone book. You might want to give a lesson on how to use the yellow pages.

An Important Call
Page 29

Goal: Read a model job-search phone conversation

Students also complete a network card for Juan, the story character.

Using the Want Ads

Page 30

Goal: Decipher and understand want ads

Students study how want ads are written. The list of common abbreviations will help students read the ads.

Want Ad Practice

Pages 31–33

Goal: Practice reading and evaluating want ads

Students are asked to find want ads for their own job interests. You may want to provide the local newspaper for students.

Learning About Job Openings

Page 34

Goal: Reflect on information learned in Unit Two

● Group Activity: Networking

Goal: Begin to build a network

Networks and personal contacts are often the most effective ways to find a job. However, because networks typically expand beyond immediate acquaintances, some students may feel uncomfortable about using a network. This group activity will help alleviate that discomfort.

Materials

Each student will need

■ a piece of blank posterboard or any large piece of blank paper

■ a felt-tip marker

■ masking tape or thumbtacks

Time Required

This activity will take about 45 minutes.

Process

Make sure the concept of how networks operate is clear.

An option is to wait until all students have explained their job interests, then to have them write information on each other's boards.

1. Review networks and their value in finding job openings. Tell students that they are going to help each other develop their own networks.

2. Tell each student to write his or her job interest (e.g., appliance repair) at the top of the posterboard, using a felt-tip marker so that it can be easily read. Then have students tape their posterboards onto the wall and explain, one at a time, the kind of job they want. The class can ask questions if necessary.

3. When the first student posts his or her job and explains it to the class, tell the other students that they will now serve as a network to help the student find job openings. Ask if any members of the class can help the student locate job openings. They may know of job openings, companies that may be hiring, or people who may be able to help. As they volunteer this information, the student can write it on his or her posterboard.

Remind students to continue to build their networks.

4. Explain that the information just gathered is an example of how to get information or job leads from a network. Emphasize that in order for the network to be helpful, students must follow up by contacting the people or organizations listed on their posterboards.

You may also have one large job posting board where students can post any job information (e.g., a want ad) they think may interest someone in the class.

5. Ask students if they would like to leave the posterboards posted so that classmates can add further information.

6. Close the activity by discussing what students have learned, what their next steps may be, and the value of networking.

● Introduction

In Unit Two, students learned where and how to find openings for their ideal jobs. This unit will help students prepare for initial formal contacts with potential employers.

Students have learned a great deal about their strengths as workers. They must understand that a potential employer will only know as much about them as they disclose. There are four primary means by which they can tell employers about themselves: a resume, a cover letter, a job application, and a job interview. The resume and the cover letter are the focus of this unit.

Many of the jobs students will apply for may not require a resume. However, the information contained in the resume will be needed to write cover letters, to fill out applications, and to interview effectively. In this unit, therefore, students will compile a complete personal and job history and will then construct a resume. The personal history will not only help students write a resume but will also contain the kinds of information needed for all steps of the application process.

Skills Used

Students will be using reading and writing skills in this unit. They will also use the critical-thinking skills of analysis and evaluation.

CASAS Objectives Addressed

4.1.2 Interpret job applications, resumes, and letters of application

4.1.6 Interpret general work-related vocabulary (e.g., experience, swing shift)

4.1.8 Identify appropriate skills and education for getting a job in various occupational areas

JTPA Checklists Addressed

Checklists A, B, C
Department of Labor Pre-Employment Skills:
1. Making Career Decisions
2. Using Labor Market Information
3. Preparing Resumes
6. Writing Cover Letter

Vocabulary

The following words used in Unit Three are important to the concepts presented, but students may find them unfamiliar and difficult to read. You may wish to teach these words at the start of this unit to help students with the activities.

- **cover letter**—a letter of application that aims to persuade an employer to read an attached resume

- **personal history**—an informal compilation of a person's work-related experiences that should emphasize strengths and successes. Pertinent experience includes education, paid work, military, volunteer, family, and free-time experiences.

- **references**—people such as past employers or teachers who can attest to a job applicant's character or work performance. References should not be family members.

- **resume**—a detailed, written summary of a job applicant's background and qualifications. In this series, the resume featured is a *skills resume*.

- **volunteer work**—work that does not provide a salary but which can provide valuable skills and experiences

● Unit Three Activities: Tips and Explanations

Your Personal History

Pages 36–43

Goal: Identify work-related skills accumulated from past experiences

Students will be reflecting on their education, paid work, military, volunteer, family, and free-time experiences. They will identify their skills that can transfer to their current job interest. In addition, students will identify their five greatest strengths and include them in a short description about themselves.

A story within this activity helps demonstrate skills learned in volunteer and family experiences.

Encourage students to take their time and answer each question. Students may need help writing their answers.

Starting Your Resume

Pages 44–45

Goal: Use information from personal history to begin a resume

In this exercise, students choose what information to include on their resume and write it under five general headings.

The resume style used in this series is an open-ended skills resume. This kind of resume is well-suited to students with little education or training to highlight. Gathering information for the resume will help students mentally prepare for the interview. To familiarize students with the skills resume format, show them the sample resume on page 46.

If your students need a more sophisticated style of resume, please consult one of the many resume books available in your library.

Sample Resume

Goal: Examine and evaluate a resume that includes little paid work experience

This sample resume demonstrates how students can emphasize their strongest areas (and downplay their weakest) on a resume. This resume emphasizes Jolyn's strengths and volunteer experiences.

Your Resume

Goal: Decide which resume format will emphasize strengths and write rough draft of resume

You may need to help students proofread these drafts. We suggest that students rewrite the information on another piece of paper. In addition, we suggest that the final versions of students' resumes be typed and photocopied.

Yvette's Cover Letter

Goal: Examine a model cover letter

Writing Your Cover Letter

Goal: Write a cover letter

Students can write the letter based on the ad provided or based on a want ad they find themselves. You may want to provide a newspaper.

What Have You Learned?

Goal: Reflect on information learned in Unit Three

☾ Group Activity: Unusual Jobs

Goal: Communicate information about job-related experiences

Note: We recommend that you conduct this activity after students complete the personal history and before they begin their resumes. This activity works best when more than eight students participate.

As students conduct their job searches, they must be sure to communicate relevant information to prospective employers. This activity is lighthearted yet serves two useful purposes: students interact with each other, and they learn to communicate information about their experiences. Students can discuss either paid or unpaid work experiences.

Materials
Each student will need

■ a pen or pencil

■ a blank sheet of paper

■ completed personal history (pages 36–43 in *Book Two*)

■ a copy of *Guess Who?* (A blackline master of this form is located on page 66 in this book.)

■ masking tape or thumbtacks

Time Required
This activity will take from 30 to 45 minutes, depending on the size of the class.

Process

You may want to tell about an unusual job you once had.

1. Ask students to think about the most unusual job they ever had, paid or unpaid. It might have been a summer job when they were in school or even a temporary job, but it should be a job others might be surprised to learn they had ever held.

   If students have trouble finding a job to use, suggest they review pages 37–41 of their Personal History.

You may need to move around the room and help students with these descriptions.

2. Ask students to describe that unusual job on the *Guess Who?* form. Tell them to include details about the job but not to write anything that might identify themselves. Students may want to disguise their handwriting, if possible.

3. When everyone has finished, collect all the forms. Number the forms and post them in random order.

4. Tell the students to take out a sheet of paper and number it from 1 to whatever number of forms is posted.

Demonstrate the process. Read one form aloud, and ask the class whose they think it is.

5. Tell students to read all of the forms and then try to decide which student worked at each job. Have them write the student's name on their numbered sheet of paper beside the same number that appears on the top of the form.

As students guess the student who held the job, ask what clues they saw in the descriptions.

6. Reconvene the class. Then, beginning with the form numbered 1, read the job description aloud and ask for volunteers to identify who they think the mystery writer might be. When he or she is identified, write the student's name on the top of the form. Continue until all the forms have been read and identified.

● Introduction

In this unit, students will bridge the gap between preparing to apply for a job and actually initiating the application process. This unit guides students through the process of completing a job application.

Completing a company's standard job application form is the most common method of applying for a job. In order for students to have all the necessary information at hand when they apply, they will develop a practice application, which contains all essential information. Students can take their practice applications with them whenever they may need to fill out an application.

This unit will also focus on the importance of accuracy, neatness, and clarity in making a good impression.

Skills Used

Students will be using reading and writing skills in this unit. They will also use the critical-thinking skills of analysis and evaluation.

CASAS Objectives Addressed

4.1.2 Interpret job applications, resumes, and letters of application

4.1.6 Interpret general work-related vocabulary (e.g., experience, swing shift)

4.1.8 Identify appropriate skills and education for getting a job in various occupational areas

JTPA Checklists Addressed

Checklists A, D

Department of Labor Pre-Employment Skills:

1. Making Career Decisions

2. Using Labor Market Information

4. Filling Out Applications

Vocabulary

The following words used in Unit Four are important to the concepts presented, but students may find them unfamiliar and difficult to read. You may wish to teach these words at the start of this unit to help students with the activities.

- **application**—a form which asks personal and work-related information of job applicants
- **practice application**—a prototype of a typical application for employment. Students can use it as a reference when they fill out actual job applications.

● Unit Four Activities: Tips and Explanations

Filling Out Your Practice Application

Page 54

Goal: Learn correct way to fill out practice application

It is important that students become familiar with using a pencil on a practice application, then transferring information in pen onto the application they plan to submit. This is a very helpful method for new readers.

You may want to add other comments about your own experiences with filling out applications.

Following Directions

Page 55

Goal: Learn to read instructions thoroughly

The character in the drawing models the consequences of not following directions.

Practice Application

Pages 56-59

Goal: Fill out a practice application

This application includes most of the commonly used items on employment applications. Once the application is complete, students can tear the page out and fold it according to the instructions. Students then will have a sample application to take along for reference when filling out a real one.

A Real Application

Pages 60-62

Goal: Fill out a copy of a Marriott Corporation application

The instructions on page 60 give tips on how to fill out this application. Most of the instructions for the practice application pertain to this one as well (i.e., use of NA). You may want to have students bring in other real applications for you to photocopy and provide for class practice.

Just for Fun

Page 63

Goal: Strengthen awareness of employment-search vocabulary

Students may need guidance in completing the crossword puzzle. Answers are shown below.

Application Know-How

Page 64

Goal: Describe a problem with filling out job applications and a way to combat the problem

◑ Group Activity: Applications

Goal: Learn the importance of completing job applications neatly and carefully

Note: We recommend that you conduct this activity after students have finished the Practice Application on pages 57–58.

No matter how strong a job candidate's qualifications are, a sloppy job application will work against the person. This activity uses the feedback of peers to encourage students to fill out applications with care.

Materials
Each student will need

■ a pen *and* pencil

■ a blank sheet of paper

■ two copies of *Sample Job Application* (A blackline master of this form is located on pages 67–68 in this book.)

■ his or her completed Personal History (pages 36–43)

■ masking tape or thumbtacks

Time Required
This activity will take from 45 to 60 minutes, depending on the size of the class.

Process

1. Give each student two copies of *Sample Job Application*. Ask students to complete one of the forms using a pencil but not to write their names on it.

Tell students to complete this application as if they were actually submitting it to an employer.

2. After students have finished the first application, ask them to look it over and make revisions. Next, have them complete the second form by copying the information from the first application; this time they should use a pen. Again, they should not write their names.

3. Collect all the forms—both pencil and ink copies. Number the forms and post them in random order on the wall.

Before students begin, discuss what they might look for (e.g., neatness, thoroughness, legibility).

4. Tell students to look at all of the application forms posted on the wall. Based on the *appearance* of the application forms (not qualifications), they should decide who would be selected for an interview. Ask them to write the numbers of the best-looking applications.

Let the authors remain anonymous if they so choose. Keep criticism constructive.

5. Reconvene the class. Look at application 1 and ask how many students would invite this applicant for an interview. Discuss the reasons why or why not. Be sure to point out the strong points of each application. Then move on to the next application.

Ask students if they would like the application forms to be posted for a while.

6. Close this activity with a discussion of the importance of doing a careful job when completing an application form.

● Introduction

In this unit, students will learn to interview effectively for a job. After students have completed this unit, they will be better prepared to meet prospective employers. They will know what to expect, and they will have practiced some of the scenarios they may encounter.

The interview is the final step in the job application process. It creates the most anxiety of any step. Much of this anxiety is a result of feeling out of control. To perform well in an interview—to maintain control—means to have an idea of what to expect and to prepare well. Helping students get ready to make the best possible impression in interviews is the focus of this unit.

Skills Used

Students will be using reading and writing skills in this unit. They will also use the critical-thinking skills of analysis and evaluation.

CASAS Objectives Addressed

4.1.5 Recognize standards of behavior for job interviews and select appropriate questions and responses during job interviews

4.1.6 Interpret general work-related vocabulary (e.g., experience, swing shift)

4.1.8 Identify appropriate skills and education for getting a job in various occupational areas

JTPA Checklists Addressed

Checklists A, E

Department of Labor Pre-Employment Skills:

1. Making Career Decisions

2. Using Labor Market Information

5. Interviewing

Vocabulary

The following words used in Unit Five are important to the concepts presented, but students may find them unfamiliar and difficult to read. You may wish to teach these words at the start of this unit to help students with the activities.

■ **eye contact**—looking straight at the person you are speaking to; an important element in interpersonal communication

■ **interview**—a meeting between an employer and a job applicant to determine an applicant's suitability for a job

■ **open-ended question**—a subjective question that has no definitive answer. This type of question is often asked in interviews and is an opportunity for the applicant to focus on strengths.

■ **thank-you note**—a letter of appreciation sent by an applicant to the person (or persons) who conducted the interview

Unit Five Activities: Tips and Explanations

Before the Interview
Page 66　　　　**Goal:** Learn how to prepare for a job interview

At the Interview
Page 67　　　　**Goal:** Become familiar with interview *do's* and *don'ts*

Picture Perfect
Page 68　　　　**Goal:** Evaluate good and poor interview behavior

Answering Questions
Page 69　　　　**Goal:** Prepare to answer open-ended interview questions

Students learn about open-ended questions. They also encounter questions that have a deeper meaning than they appear to have. Emphasize that students should always focus on their strengths in interviews.

Handling a Tough Question
Pages 70–71　　　　**Goal:** Prepare to answer interview questions about work performance

Again, emphasize to students that they should focus on their strengths.

Be Confident
Page 72　　　　**Goal:** Prepare to answer interview questions evaluating self-confidence

After students complete this page, you might ask the class to come up with other tough interview questions not mentioned in the student book.

You Be the Interviewer
Page 73　　　　**Goal:** Learn to ask questions at a job interview

You may want to help students think of additional questions.

Hiring Me Will Help You!

Page 74

Goal: Summarize information a candidate should present and obtain at a job interview

Thank You

Page 75

Goal: Become familiar with the thank-you note

Practice Interview

Pages 76–77

Goal: Practice a job interview

In addition to instructions, an interview rating sheet is provided to facilitate feedback.

You Can Do It!

Page 78

Goal: Describe an interviewing problem and a way to solve the problem

This is a summary activity for the unit. It asks students to describe what concerns them most about being interviewed. Students then reflect on ways to deal with these concerns.

◕ Group Activity: Interviewing

Goal: Realize the value of preparing for an interview and practice an interview

Note: We recommend that you conduct this activity after students have finished the Practice Interview on pages 76–77.

In this activity, students will practice answering some typical job-interview questions but in a nonthreatening setting. There are several benefits to this activity: it allows students to actually respond to interview questions, it helps students see the value of preparing for anticipated questions, and it allows students to receive feedback on their performance. While not as stressful or extensive as a real interview, this simulation should help students become better prepared for the real thing.

Materials

Each student will need

■ a copy of *Interview Questions* (A blackline master of this form is located on page 69 in this book.)

Time Required

This activity will take about 60 minutes. The amount of time will vary according to the size of the class and how much discussion is appropriate after the interviews have been completed.

It is important to demonstrate the interview simulation. Ask two students to assist you: one to interview you, and the other to observe.

In your demonstration, tell the class how you are thinking through your responses. After the interview, help the third student provide feedback.

Process

1. Form small groups of three students each. Explain that students are going to practice responding to interview questions. One student will be interviewed by a second student. The third student will watch and listen; after the interview, he or she will give feedback to the student who was interviewed. The process is repeated until each student has played all three roles.

2. Pass out the *Interview Questions* forms. Explain that the interviewer will select three of the five questions listed on the form to ask in the interview. The person being interviewed is given a few minutes to think about how to answer them. Remind students that this extra time won't be available in a real interview.

3. After all three interviews have been completed, reconvene the class. Ask students to talk about what it was like to answer these questions. The following questions may be helpful in leading the discussion:

   - *"How did you prepare the answers you were going to use?"*

   - *"What difficulties did you have?"*

   - *"Do you feel better prepared for a real interview?"*

   - *"Do you have any actual interview experiences that you would like to share with the class?"*

   - *"Are there any interview questions that you're not sure how to answer?"*

◑ Introduction

This is the final unit of the *You're Hired!* series. Up to this point, students have been through an extensive process of self-assessment, job assessment, and job-search steps. This unit departs from all previous ones by helping students learn how to manage themselves after they have a job. Students will look at factors that help them keep a job, be successful on the job, and get ahead.

This unit also addresses the important concept of employee rights and responsibilities. The issue of discrimination is complicated and technical and can only be lightly addressed in this unit.

In addition, Unit Six focuses on job evaluation and problem solving. Many students are not aware of the standard probationary period and the performance review following that period. The job evaluation often highlights an employee's poor performance areas. This unit helps students identify and solve these problems.

Finally, this unit distinguishes between "getting by" and "getting ahead." To get by, workers need to meet minimal expectations. Getting ahead, however, requires greater effort and action. Students may choose whether they want to get by or get ahead, but they need to understand the difference.

Skills Used

Students will be using reading and writing skills in this unit. They will also use critical-thinking and problem-solving skills.

CASAS Objectives Addressed

4.3.3 Identify safe work procedures including wearing safe work attire

4.4.1 Identify appropriate behavior, attitudes, and social interaction for keeping a job and getting a promotion

4.4.2 Identify appropriate skills and education for keeping a job and getting a promotion

4.4.5 Interpret tasks related to clarifying, giving, or providing feedback to instructions; and reacting to criticism

JTPA Checklists Addressed

Checklist F

Department of Labor Work Maturity Skills:

7. Being Consistently Punctual

8. Maintaining Regular Attendance

10. Demonstrating Positive Attitudes/Behaviors

12. Completing Tasks Effectively

Vocabulary

The following words used in Unit Six are important to the concepts presented, but students may find them unfamiliar and difficult to read. You may wish to teach these words at the start of this unit to help students with the activities.

- **discrimination**—a difference in treatment on a basis other than individual merit; for instance, on the basis of race, religion, national origin, ancestry, age, sex, or disability

- **expectations**—things that an employer asks of an employee, such as putting in a full day's work for a full day's pay

- **probation**—in this series, *probation* refers to the time during which a new employee's performance will be observed to determine if he or she is capable of doing the work

- **regular employee**—an employee who has passed the probationary period on a job and is entitled to full benefits

- **responsibilities**—things that a person is obligated to accomplish or adhere to. In this series, *responsibilities* refers to both employer and employee accountability.

- **rights**—standards of personal and professional treatment and working conditions that are dictated by law and apply equally to all citizens. In this series, *rights* refers to employees' rights against discrimination.

◓ Unit Six Activities: Tips and Explanations

Al's Story

Pages 80-81

Goal: Read about an employee's first day at work

This story introduces the concept of probation period and points out the different forms and information a new employee receives.

Your Rights

Page 82

Goal: Understand the meaning of *equal opportunity* and *discrimination*

Where to Get Help

Pages 83-84

Goal: Locate the nearest Equal Employment Opportunity Commission office

Responsibilities

Page 85

Goal: Distinguish between responsibilities of employee and employer

The word *company* is used for employer here to help students distinguish responsibilities. This activity might make a good class discussion topic. Students may think of other responsibilities as well.

Al Makes the Grade

Pages 86–87

Goal: Become familiar with the performance review

Students will also evaluate the story character's performance review and focus on the area that needs the most work.

Al Takes Action

Pages 88–89

Goal: Read about and evaluate positive steps taken to improve poor work review areas

Students answer one question about the story and then consider a work-related problem they need to solve. This is also a good discussion topic.

Getting Ahead

Pages 90–91

Goal: Examine how an employee shows he wants to get ahead

Students are asked to pair up to discuss what Al needs to do. You may want to follow with a class discussion.

Congratulations!

Page 92

Goal: Review information learned in *Book Two* and plan how to use this information in the future

Certificate

Blackline Master

You may wish to recognize the completion of *Book Two* with an award. You may choose an award of your own or use the certificate we have included as a blackline master on page 63 of this guide.

◑ Group Activity: On-the-Job Problems

Goal: Think about problems encountered at the workplace and consider appropriate ways to deal with them

In this activity, students are presented with brief work scenarios and then given the opportunity to discuss the problems and possible solutions with their classmates. While there is no right answer to any of these situations, thinking about them and talking them over may help students deal with similar problems they may encounter.

Problems presented are representative of the many real-world problems of the workplace.

Materials

Each student will need

■ one copy of *Work Problems* (A blackline master of this form is located on page 70 in this book.)

Time Required

This activity will take about 45 minutes. The amount of time will vary according to the size of the class and how much discussion is appropriate after the interviews have been completed.

Process

1. Ask students to think about some problem or difficult situation they have encountered at work. Ask for volunteers to describe the situation, how they were involved, and what happened.

Demonstrate this process and emphasize that the discussion not become negative. If students begin complaining about an employer or a job, discuss possible solutions to the problem.

2. Pick one of the situations described by a student or pick one of the scenarios from *Work Problems*. Make sure the class understands the situation, and discuss it with the whole class by addressing each of the three questions on *Work Problems*:

   • Why is this a problem?

   • Whose problem is it?

   • What could be done to solve the problem?

Tell students that they will discuss these scenarios as a class when the small groups have finished.

3. Form small groups of two to five students. Pass out copies of *Work Problems* to each student. Four scenarios are listed on the form. You can have students work on any or all of the scenarios, depending on their interest and the time available.

   Have them read the scenarios and ask questions if they do not understand any part of them. Then tell each group to select a scenario. Each member of the group should write a short answer to the three questions that follow.

Remind them to stay on task during their discussions.

4. Now tell each group to discuss the questions, using their individual answers to guide them.

During the class discussion, ask students to put themselves in the place of the employer. How would the problem and the solution look to them then?

5. Reconvene the class. Ask which groups discussed the first scenario. Ask for a volunteer group to talk about the scenario and the solutions they discussed.

   Have the whole class decide which solutions would work the best for everyone concerned. Then talk about how this activity might help students on the job.

   Finally, repeat the process for each scenario.

Bibliography

The following books may be useful references regarding the theory and practice of career development:

Anderson, Nancy. *Work with Passion: How to Do What You Love for a Living*. New York: Carroll and Graf Publishers, Inc., 1984.

Bolles, Richard N. *The Three Boxes of Life: And How to Get Out of Them*. Berkeley: Ten Speed Press, 1981.

Bolles, Richard N. *What Color Is Your Parachute?* Revised Edition. Berkeley: Ten Speed Press, 1990.

Herr, Edwin L., and Stanley H. Cramer. *Career Guidance Through the Lifespan: Systematic Approaches*. Boston: Little, Brown and Company, 1979.

Holland, John L. *Making Vocational Choices: A Theory of Careers*. Englewood Cliffs, N.J.: Prentice-Hall, 1973.

U.S. Department of Labor. Bureau of Labor Statistics. *Occupational Outlook Handbook*. Washington, D.C.: U.S. Government Printing Office (check for current edition).

U.S. Department of Labor. U.S. Employment Service. *Dictionary of Occupational Titles*. Washington, D.C.; U.S. Government Printing Office (check for current edition).

The following professional journals, available at many college libraries, are additional sources of a variety of current career information:

Journal of College Student Personnel

Journal of Counseling Psychology

Journal of Employment Counseling

Journal of Vocational Behavior

Vocational Guidance Quarterly

CERTIFICATE OF ACHIEVEMENT

AWARDED TO

FOR SUCCESSFULLY COMPLETING

You're Hired!

Book One: Charting Your Career Path

DATE

INSTRUCTOR'S SIGNATURE

☐   ☐   ☐   ☐   ☐

Personal Values

1. Read all the values on this page.

2. Put an X next to the five values most important to you.

3. Number the values you marked with an X from 1 to 5: put number 1 by the value most important to you, number 2 by the value second most important to you, and so on.

4. Look at each of the five values you chose. Is it fulfilled in your life? If so, write YES next to it. If not, write NO next to it.

Values	5 most important (X)	How important? (1-5)	Fulfilled? (YES or NO)
Be free to do what I enjoy			
Be happy			
Sense inner peace			
Feel good about myself			
Have good health			
Be liked by others			
Have fun in my life			
Have no worries about money			
Know I did well			
Have lots of free time			
Be in good shape			
Be loving			
Be kind to others			
Be in charge of my own life			
Be honest			
Do what I know I should			
Have others respect me			
Live in a certain part of the country			
Have an open mind			
Be neat			
Take risks			
Have time to think			
Be artistic			

| | ☐ | ☐ | ☐ | ☐ | ☐ |

 # Work Values

1. Read all the values on this page.

2. Put an X next to the five values most important to you.

3. Number the values you marked with an X from 1 to 5: put number 1 by the value most important to you, number 2 by the value second most important to you, and so on.

4. Look at each of the five values you chose. Is it fulfilled in your life? If so, write YES next to it. If not, write NO next to it.

Values	5 most important (X)	How important? (1-5)	Fulfilled? (YES or NO)
Have steady work			
Earn good money			
Work indoors			
Work outdoors			
Travel			
Work the same hours every day			
Have friends on the job			
Have a good boss			
Help others			
Be part of a team			
Learn new things			
Know what they want me to do			
Work flexible hours			
Be in charge			
Do or make something important			
Work with people			
Feel good about my work			
Work close to home			
Do one thing at a time			
Work in my own way			
Stay busy			
Work by myself			
Do clean work			
Get ahead in my job			
Have health insurance			
Have vacation and sick days			
Do many different things			
Use what I already know			

	□	□	□	□	□

 # People Values

1. Read all the values on this page.

2. Put an X next to the five values most important to you.

3. Number the values you marked with an X from 1 to 5: put number 1 by the value most important to you, number 2 by the value second most important to you, and so on.

4. Look at the five values you chose. Is it fulfilled in your life? If so, write YES next to it. If not, write NO next to it.

Values	5 most important (X)	How important? (1-5)	Fulfilled? (YES or NO)
Have lots of friends			
Have close family ties			
Know lots of people			
Have a good, solid marriage			
Have someone to turn to or talk to			
Make friends			
Be needed			
Have a few close friends			
Have a family nearby			
Have time to be alone			
Know people I can trust			
Have a great social life			
Spend money on my friends			
Have someone to do things with			
Be a good friend			
Be a good parent			
Be a good son or daughter			
Help others			
Meet new people			
Be independent			

□   □   □   □   □

◪ Personal Accomplishment

Describe something you have accomplished that you are proud of:

_____

_____

_____

_____

_____

_____

List the Everyday Skills that helped you to be successful.

_____   _____

_____   _____

_____   _____

_____   _____

_____   _____

_____   _____

_____   _____

List the Job Skills that helped you to be successful.

☐   ☐   ☐   ☐   ☐

▢ My Interests

By answering the questions on pages 56–59, you may discover some of your everyday interests—things you enjoy doing outside of work. Answer at least one question on each page.

Wishes—things you hope for or dream about

1. What things do you daydream about doing?

_____

_____

_____

2. If you had a year to do whatever you wanted and nothing to stop you, such as family or lack of money, what would you do?

_____

_____

_____

3. Do you have a dream job? What is it?

_____

_____

_____

☐   ☐   ☐   ☐   ☐

◰ My Interests

Activities—things you enjoy doing

1. What do you really enjoy doing in your free time?

_____

_____

_____

2. What are some of the most enjoyable things you have ever done?

_____

_____

_____

3. What is the best job you ever had, either paid or as a volunteer?

_____

_____

_____

☐   ☐   ☐   ☐   ☐

■ My Interests

Attractions—things that appeal to you

1. What person do you admire the most? Why?

_____

_____

_____

2. What things do you most look forward to doing?

_____

_____

_____

3. Do people you know have jobs that seem great to you? What kind of jobs are they?

_____

_____

_____

☐	☐	☐	☐	☐

Job Family #_____ _____	MY VALUES	First Job Interest _____
Personal	1	◯
	2	◯
	3	◯
	4	◯
	5	◯
Work	1	◯
	2	◯
	3	◯
	4	◯
	5	◯
People	1	◯
	2	◯
	3	◯
	4	◯
	5	◯
How all of my VALUES match this Job Interest		◯
	MY SKILLS	
Everyday	1	◯
	2	◯
	3	◯
	4	◯
	5	◯
Job	1	◯
	2	◯
	3	◯
	4	◯
How all of my SKILLS match this Job Interest		◯

Second Job Interest	Third Job Interest
1 ◯	◯
2 ◯	◯
3 ◯	◯
4 ◯	◯
5 ◯	◯
1 ◯	◯
2 ◯	◯
3 ◯	◯
4 ◯	◯
5 ◯	◯
1 ◯	◯
2 ◯	◯
3 ◯	◯
4 ◯	◯
5 ◯	◯
◯	◯
1 ◯	◯
2 ◯	◯
3 ◯	◯
4 ◯	◯
5 ◯	◯
1 ◯	◯
2 ◯	◯
3 ◯	◯
4 ◯	◯
◯	◯

Sample: Which Jobs Fit You Best?

Values
- sense of inner peace
- help others
- be a part of a team

Job Interests
- teacher aide
- caseworker
- flight attendant

Skills
- meet people easily
- explain things clearly
- plan my work

Jobs

1. run a daycare center
2. be a kindergarten teacher
3. be a licensed practical nurse
4. be an activities director at a children's camp
5. be an employment counselor

Which Jobs Fit You Best?

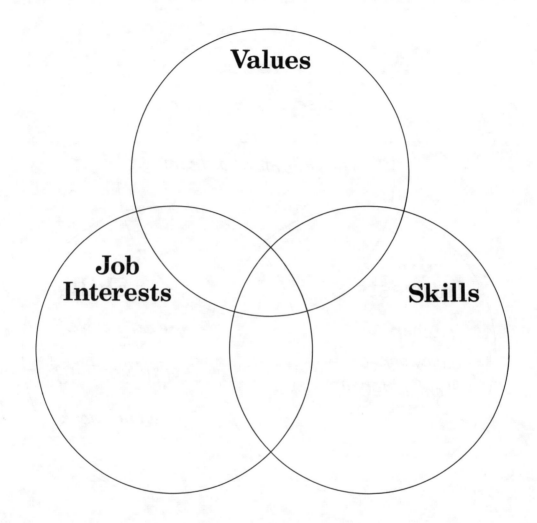

Jobs

1. _____

2. _____

3. _____

4. _____

5. _____

CERTIFICATE OF ACHIEVEMENT

AWARDED TO

FOR SUCCESSFULLY COMPLETING

You're Hired!

Book Two: Getting the Right Job

DATE   INSTRUCTOR'S SIGNATURE

◑ Job Information

General Information

1. What was your job title? _____

2. What company did you work for? _____

3. How long did you work there? _____

4. How did you get the job? _____

Job Description

5. Tell about your job, including the kinds of tasks you did in a normal day.

_____

_____

_____

6. What skills did you need to do the job?

_____

_____

7. How did you learn those skills? _____

_____

8. What days and hours did you work? _____

_____

9. What was the pay range? _____

10. Did you have a chance to get promoted? _____

Personal Views

11. What did you like about the job? _____

_____

12. What did you dislike about the job? _____

_____

◖ Network Sheet

You may use this sheet to keep track of all the contacts you make. Be sure to keep all your network sheets together in a notebook.

Who to contact _____	Who to contact _____
What company _____	What company _____
Phone number _____	Phone number _____
Referred by _____	Referred by _____
After the contact: What to do next	**After the contact:** What to do next
Who to contact _____	Who to contact _____
What company _____	What company _____
Phone number _____	Phone number _____
Referred by _____	Referred by _____
After the contact: What to do next	**After the contact:** What to do next
Who to contact _____	Who to contact _____
What company _____	What company _____
Phone number _____	Phone number _____
Referred by _____	Referred by _____
After the contact: What to do next	**After the contact:** What to do next

◗ Guess Who?

Job Title: _____

Employer: _____

In the space below, describe the kind of work you did on this job. Include details of the tasks you carried out.

_____

_____

_____

_____

_____

_____

_____

_____

_____

_____

_____

_____

● Sample Job Application

Personal Information	
PRINT NAME (Last)　　　　　(First)　　　　　(Middle)	DATE
	SOCIAL SECURITY #
ADDRESS (Number and Street)	TELEPHONE
(City)　　　　　(State)　　　　　(Zip Code) ☐ YES CITIZEN OF THE U.S.? ☐ NO If NO, are you legally allowed to work in the U.S.?	☐ YES ☐ NO Write registration number here

Job Interest

POSITION DESIRED	SALARY EXPECTED	DATE AVAILABLE

Education

	SCHOOL NAME	ADDRESS	MAJOR STUDIES	DEGREE(S)	DATES ATTENDED
HIGH SCHOOL					
COLLEGE					
BUSINESS or VOCATIONAL					

OTHER SPECIAL KNOWLEDGE OR SKILLS

Work History

List all employment, starting with your most recent employer. Include job-related volunteer work.

DATES OF EMPLOYMENT	EMPLOYER NAME AND ADDRESS	JOB TITLE AND DUTIES	NAME OF SUPERVISOR	REASON FOR LEAVING	HIGHEST SALARY

PRACTICE APPLICATION (continued)				
Military				
BRANCH OF U.S. SERVICE	DATE ENTERED	DATE DISCHARGED	FINAL RANK	TYPE DISCHARGE
Office Skills				

Office Skills

Do you type? ☐ YES If YES, WPM _____
☐ NO

WHAT OFFICE MACHINES
CAN YOU OPERATE?

Other Information

HAVE YOU EVER BEEN CONVICTED OF A FELONY? ☐ YES If YES, please explain
☐ NO

Personal References

List the names and phone numbers of three references. No relatives please.

NAME	ADDRESS	PHONE

I swear all statements in this application are true and correct. I understand that any false answers will be cause for dismissal if I am hired. I give permission for the investigation of all statements in this application. This includes contacting former employers.

Signature of Applicant _____

☉ Interview Questions

Choose three of the following questions to ask in the interview.

Questions

1. What did you like best about your last job?

2. What is your greatest strength and greatest weakness?

3. Tell me about your work history.

4. What was your last boss or supervisor like?

5. What do you want to be doing five years from now?

◖ Work Problems

1. You and a co-worker are working on a project. You are both responsible for getting the job done. The person working with you is goofing off and not doing his share of the work. The boss was expecting the project to be done by now, but it isn't ready. The boss will be here in 10 minutes.

    - Why is this a problem?

    - Whose problem is it?

    - What could be done to solve the problem?

2. Your supervisor has asked you to work late. There is a very important project that has to be done tomorrow. You would not mind working late most days, but you have a very important date tonight.

    - Why is this a problem?

    - Whose problem is it?

    - What could be done to solve the problem?

3. You have two supervisors. One has told you to work at the front desk, which is your usual job. Five minutes later the other supervisor says a delivery has just arrived and she needs your help in the storeroom. There is no one else to cover the front desk.

    - Why is this a problem?

    - Whose problem is it?

    - What could be done to solve the problem?

4. You find out that a co-worker has been telling lies about you at work. You have to work with this person today.

    - Why is this a problem?

    - Whose problem is it?

    - What could be done to solve the problem?